"'Remember that you are meant to be here. / You must allow yourself to exist / in whatever way you have arrived to the space.' This was an invitation I received upon entering Rob Macaisa Colgate's *Hardly Creatures*, a collection unlike any I have ever encountered before. Part primer, part activated art space, part personal/community inventory, part lyric collaboration with mental illness—this book activates new zones between disability studies and poetry, allowing readers spaces for rest, recognition, and reimagination inside its dazzling and varied forms. An extraordinary document in care, mutual aid, and access that positions the self (all selves) as existing inside a network of interdependence."

—Claudia Rankine,
author of *Citizen*

"'Decide to not always be ok— / you are a creature. You need rhythms. You need to // Dance.' Never before have I experienced a book of poems that cares this firmly and boldly, this inventively and fully, for its communities and for its reader. Care as in curation, as in accessibility, as in a lover's touch, as in impromptu feast or imperfect dance floor, as in queer disabled politics and poetics in true—and often, very funny—practice. There is such space (sometimes literal, physical space) in these pages to pause, to rest, to giggle and/or sob, before engaging once again with yet another 'fabulous intensity.' Like the best art galleries, by the end I didn't want to leave and I couldn't wait to get back home, thoroughly changed. Moving through *Hardly Creatures*, Rob Macaisa Colgate's brilliant debut, I felt my entire world shift, soften, begin to glow, 'each mote of glow / lifting me, cell by cell—'."

—Chen Chen,
author of *Your Emergency Contact Has Experienced an Emergency*

"Rob Macaisa Colgate's *Hardly Creatures* is a stunning and tender portal into an accessible art gallery, full of vulnerability and humor and lyrical play and messiness and hopescrolling. These poems live in crip time, with benches and pages to say 'slow down. No poem on this page.' In this speculative space of the gallery, there is such radical realness—tending to mental health, queer love, the selves, and beloveds in the disability community. Woven with inventive form, these poems reimagine abecedarians alongside work email translations. Each poem dwells to the visceral complexities of care; they declare: 'No / body / is useless.' *Hardly Creatures* is a beautiful space I want to return to again and again. I want to go to Seafood City after reading these poems, want to be the butterfly a shorebird dips into water, want to teach this book immediately, want to touch these poems and linger alongside each 'mote of glow / lifting me, cell by cell—'."

—**Jane Wong**,
author of *Meet Me Tonight in Atlantic City*

Hardly Creatures

Hardly Creatures

poems

Rob Macaisa Colgate

TIN HOUSE
PORTLAND, OREGON

First US Edition 2025
Printed in the United States of America

EPIGRAPH CREDIT: Excerpt from "Against Access" by John Lee Clark,
from *McSweeney's* Issue 64, copyright 2021 by John Lee Clark.

SYMBOL CREDIT: The KultureCity logo is used by permission of KultureCity, Inc.

Manufacturing by Kingery Printing Company
Interior design by Beth Steidle

Library of Congress Cataloging-in-Publication Data

Names: Colgate, Rob Macaisa, author.
Title: Hardly creatures : poems / Rob Macaisa Colgate.
Description: Portland, Oregon : Tin House, 2025.
Identifiers: LCCN 2024051551 | ISBN 9781963108248 (paperback) |
ISBN 9781963108323 (ebook)
Subjects: LCGFT: Poetry.
Classification: LCC PS3603.O4375 H37 2025 | DDC 811/.6—dc23/eng/20241118
LC record available at https://lccn.loc.gov/2024051551

Tin House
2617 NW Thurman Street
Portland, OR 97210
www.tinhouse.com

DISTRIBUTED BY W. W. NORTON & COMPANY
1 2 3 4 5 6 7 8 9 0

WRITTEN ON THE LAND OF THE ABENAKI & ANISHINAABE & CHIPPEWA & HAUDENOSAUNEE & MISSISSAUGAS OF THE CREDIT & WENDAT & ABENAKI & ANISHINAABE & CHIPPEWA & HAUDENOSAUNEE & MISSISSAUGAS OF THE CREDIT & WENDAT & ABENAKI & ANISHINAABE & CHIPPEWA & HAUDENOSAUNEE & MISSISSAUGAS OF THE CREDIT & WENDAT & ABENAKI & ANISHINAABE & CHIPPEWA & HAUDENOSAUNEE & MISSISSAUGAS OF THE CREDIT & WENDAT & ABENAKI & ANISHINAABE & CHIPPEWA & HAUDENOSAUNEE & MISSISSAUGAS OF THE CREDIT & WENDAT & ABENAKI & ANISHINAABE & CHIPPEWA & HAUDENOSAUNEE & MISSISSAUGAS OF THE CREDIT & WENDAT & ABENAKI & ANISHINAABE & CHIPPEWA & HAUDENOSAUNEE & MISSISSAUGAS OF THE CREDIT & WENDAT & ABENAKI & ANISHINAABE & CHIPPEWA & HAUDENOSAUNEE & MISSISSAUGAS OF THE CREDIT & WENDAT & ABENAKI & ANISHINAABE & CHIPPEWA & HAUDENOSAUNEE & MISSISSAUGAS OF THE CREDIT & WENDAT & ABENAKI & ANISHINAABE & CHIPPEWA & HAUDENOSAUNEE & MISSISSAUGAS OF THE CREDIT & WENDAT & ABENAKI & ANISHINAABE & CHIPPEWA & HAUDENOSAUNEE & MISSISSAUGAS OF THE CREDIT & WENDAT & ABENAKI & ANISHINAABE & CHIPPEWA & HAUDENOSAUNEE & MISSISSAUGAS OF THE CREDIT & WENDAT & ABENAKI & ANISHINAABE & CHIPPEWA & HAUDENOSAUNEE & MISSISSAUGAS OF THE CREDIT & WENDAT & ABENAKI & ANISHINAABE & CHIPPEWA & HAUDENOSAUNEE & MISSISSAUGAS OF THE CREDIT & WENDAT & ABENAKI & ANISHINAABE & CHIPPEWA & HAUDENOSAUNEE & MISSISSAUGAS OF THE CREDIT & WENDAT & ABENAKI & ANISHINAABE & CHIPPEWA & HAUDENOSAUNEE & MISSISSAUGAS OF THE CREDIT & WENDAT & ABENAKI & ANISHINAABE & CHIPPEWA & HAUDENOSAUNEE & MISSISSAUGAS OF THE CREDIT & WENDAT & ABENAKI & ANISHINAABE & CHIPPEWA & HAUDENOSAUNEE & MISSISSAUGAS OF THE CREDIT & WENDAT & ABENAKI & ANISHINAABE & CHIPPEWA & HAUDENOSAUNEE & MISSISSAUGAS OF THE CREDIT & WENDAT & ABENAKI & ANISHINAABE & CHIPPEWA & HAUDENOSAUNEE & MISSISSAUGAS OF THE CREDIT & WENDAT & ABENAKI & ANISHINAABE & CHIPPEWA & HAUDENOSAUNEE & MISSISSAUGAS OF THE CREDIT & WENDAT & ABENAKI & ANISHINAABE & CHIPPEWA & HAUDENOSAUNEE & MISSISSAUGAS OF THE CREDIT & WENDAT & ABENAKI & ANISHINAABE & CHIPPEWA & HAUDENOSAUNEE & MISSISSAUGAS OF THE CREDIT & WENDAT & ABENAKI & ANISHINAABE & CHIPPEWA & HAUDENOSAUNEE & MISSISSAUGAS OF THE CREDIT & WENDAT & ABENAKI & ANISHINAABE & CHIPPEWA & HAUDENOSAUNEE & MISSISSAUGAS OF THE CREDIT & WENDAT

A Gallery of Our Own

Exit: Gift Shop and Vestibule

Access Legend

Access Support Worker

Information Available

Trigger Warning

Please Touch

Sensory Sensitivity

Translation Available

Gender Inclusive Space

Physically Accessible

Audio Description

Low-Vision Guided Tour

Close Captioning

Relaxed Event

Alt Text or Visual Description

Plain Language

Assistive Tablet Available

Too often all we have, a dead end, leading nowhere:
captions without images, lyrics without music,
raised lines without color, labels without objects,
descriptions without anchors.

—John Lee Clark

Hardly Creatures

Entryway

We Do Not Enter the Gallery

Which means the docent does not look at us confused.

Heather does not fail to find instructions on touching the art.

Alex does not notice the digital tour is only available for certain artworks.

Lorraine does not struggle to read the didactic panel hung high above her chair.

The panel does not claim there is no story behind the French artist who spent
    the latter half of his life sculpting the same bronze figure over and over.

I do not start thinking about those life tasks I am stuck doing over and over,
    do not think about curating three meals or setting tomorrow's
    alarm or scheduling another appointment and paying for it.

I do not grow confused at which tasks I enjoy and which I abhor,
    which make me happy to be alive and happy to be dying.
    I do not walk in circles fluttering my hands as this happens.

I do not snap painfully back into my body after zoning out, do not feel bad
    that I am wasting my time in this gallery that I paid money to enter.

Leaving early, I do not begin to wonder what it might look like
    if my friends and I built a gallery of our own.
    I do not begin to wonder what it would feel like to belong.

I do not fail to convince myself to call Gabbie or Jody or Kurt when I start
            having a psychotic episode alone in the crowded subway station
      even though they have told me every day since I have known them
                        that I can call any of them for anything
         literally anything this is not anything none of this happens
                        none of this happens I do not
            stumble up and down the long hall of the train
                  the long haul of training to live like this I do not
                        somehow make it to my apartment I do not
         turn on the light I do not find a great emptiness waiting I do not
                        shut my eyes at the sight

Access Guide

Feel free to skip this and head right into the gallery
(page 19) if that is what feels best for you.

Guide Overview

Information

This is the space. Here is how we learn to belong in it.

Relaxed Visits: For neurodivergent gallerygoers or those sensitive to sensory output or those overwhelmingly alive.

• *Relaxed Hours:*   Come as you are—tired, or restless, or scared of bright lights— come in the night when you are somehow most awake.

• *Relaxed Seating:*   The colors and shapes will look the same from your bed, from the floor, from the train or ocean or heaven.

• *Relaxed Tour:*   Wander through the rooms in any order. You do not have to visit them all or look at every artwork.

There is no correct way to move through a house that you live in.

Access Features: Tactile replicas, alt text, transcriptions, guided tours, sensory rooms, etc. available without request or revelation that you might ever request.

Access Doula: A care attendant will check in with you about what lies ahead in each wing.

You do not need to listen to them. They are only there if you want help with listening to yourself.

Content Warnings: The attendant will raise their hand during sharper attempts at truth:

You are allowed to reach for it if you would like.

Apologies: We are sorry that the fonts are not larger.
We are sorry that the page has no texture or sound.
We wish the benches were benches instead of poems.

We understand if you have to leave
and will treasure the absence that remains.

Access Cues

Here are three strings.

~~~~~~

<><><><><><><><><><><><><><><><><><><><><><><><><><><><><><>

— —

Pick one to wrap around your finger while you are in the gallery
as a reminder to yourself of yourself.

Fuzzy string: fragile.

Braided string: recovering.

Thin string: strong.

Remember that you are meant to be here.
You must allow yourself to exist
in whatever way you have arrived to the space.

Sensory Room I

Feel free to flip back here whenever you need.
Stay as long as you want.

The light stays as dim as you would like.

I promise the light stays.

Thumb and pinky extended while moving toward self
then fingers on both hands folded toward chest
then index finger pointed up and spun in circle.

Thumb and pinky extended and hand moved down.

Hands rotated at wrist toward center of body
with third and fourth fingers folded toward body
then index finger to the lips, then flat palm pressed on top of other fist.

Index finger pointed up and away, then hands rotated at wrist
toward center of body with third and fourth fingers folded toward body.

Gender-Neutral Bathroom

Ode to Pissing

I go over to Lorraine's on Thursdays to lift her onto the toilet.
The vinyl sling creaks, sings, and for a moment, above her powerchair,
she levitates, which is usually magical, but today she is only pissing.

•

There is supposed to be something magical about pissing. All these extra-
vagant necessities: the frescoed ceiling as shelter, or singing and syrups
when we are forced to eat. There must be some melodrama left for excretion.

•

I put on *Melodrama* and lift the toilet seat to piss while the shower warms up.
Outside the bathroom, Eli flickers the lights on and off, a homemade
strobe, *just a miniature rave for you, darling,* and I listen to him sing.

•

The song of piss on porcelain. Lorraine and I talk dreams of bathhouse raves,
disabled teachers, careers in porn. I ask how she became so comfortable
with friends wiping her and she shrugs, lifts her shoulders, checks if she's done.

•

Juliana and I squeeze shoulder to shoulder into the stall at Woody's.
The muffled singing, our laughable sweat, *go piss girl,* and I lift the gloss
to her lips while she sits there, every stickiness part of the night's piss-drunk ritual.

•

Last year, in the bathroom of the library stacks, a boy whom I had never seen
piss lifted my shirt, sang his tongue down my torso, and I think
of my silence, all of the disordered words that I never put in concert for him.

•

We sing along from the concert bathroom, Clay draining his catheter
of piss, Sarah emptying her ostomy bag. We joke that this is what disabled people
do in stalls instead of coke, then Helen lifts a baggie, asks if we want any coke.

•

How Eli has to lift himself onto his toes to kiss me, how the kissing frees
my tongue of sensemaking, and before any more touching: *I have to piss first
I'm so sorry.* He grins, runs off while I queue up a song about flashing lights.

•

AWOLing the night out, I lift myself across the city, run after words
that won't walk home together. Home in the bathroom, I curl on the tile's
cold song, schizophasia babbling like piss around a drain that will not clear.

•

I think that cold part of my body that is supposed to produce shame is disabled too. I lift

my eyebrows, nod, wind toilet paper around my hand like a song on loop.
Lorraine clarifies: *I'm not just some incontinent woman. I'm a bitch who shits.*

•

Unclear when Eli found me, only that he did, only that he lifted
my body from the piss-stained floor, the Seroquel to my mouth,
and in bed he sings the lullaby out of order so I might understand the words.

•

And Lorraine tries to lift from me the shame that, for her, has lulled.
Her question: *What moment made you realize you could piss in front of Eli?*
My quiet shock. *When I couldn't speak straight, he suggested I sing.*

Accessible Transit Info

Commute

for Jordan Neely, a brother in madness

On the train home, an evangelist. He says:

> *GOD IS CALLING YOU TO COME HOME TO HIM*

My eyes closed, pretending he cannot see me on this third day
of antipsychotic withdrawal, my insurance expired, my shaking
conspicuous, visible in a city that prefers me invisible.

> *GOD IS THE ONLY CURE THE ONLY WAY OUT*

Thoughts turn to hell, its humid throng, the train forever skipping
your stop, how hell is two flights of stairs below street level
and the elevator to heaven is always out of service.

> *HE IS THINKING ABOUT YOU ALL THE TIME*

Then thoughts of Jordan, how I misheard his last name as *kneeling*.
Him on the train, kneeling, the hard pew of orange plastic,
kneeling, no seat for his body, no seat for his prayer.

> *HE IS THINKING ABOUT YOU LIKE A MANIAC LOVER*

Jordan kneeling, praying, trying to be grateful
for the unsolicited voices, for being graced by God
with more to hear than everyone else on the train.

HE IS THINKING ABOUT RIDDING YOU OF YOUR BROKEN BODY

Jordan weary, tired of squeezing his voice to his chest
in the rush hour crowd. When he finally lets his yelling go
it unfolds like an exhausted limb, and no one makes room.

HE IS ALL AROUND YOU YOU CANNOT IGNORE HIM

Jordan screaming, about how prison and death are both places
where you get to lie down, and I wish I were there to nod, and now
everyone is either staring or avoiding staring, and both feel like a slur.

HE WILL CALL AND CALL UNTIL YOU EITHER ANSWER OR DIE

Then silence. Jordan still kneeling in reverence for a voice
that, to others, is silence. A stranger kneeling on his neck, silencing him
for listening too closely to that voice, that silence, that God.

YOU ARE BREATHING HIM IN IF YOU CHOKE YOU ARE CHOKING ON GOD

The stranger doing this because it is the only way
he can imagine to silence the voice that he cannot hear,
the voice he does not want taking up a seat on the train.

GOD HAS A PLACE FOR YOU IT IS SMALL AND YOU SIT THERE FOREVER

But now I cannot keep ignoring the evangelist, his unsolicited
mistranslation of God's unsolicited voice, and how
the commuters somehow step silently aside for it.

GOD WILL NOT BE SILENT UNTIL HE IS DONE SAVING YOU

To silence this evangelist I must silence God.

DO NOT IGNORE HEAVEN CRYING IN YOUR EAR

The evangelist approaches me, eyes steady, says,

YOU KNOW GOD MADE YOU IN HIS IMAGE

He looks me up and down, sees my tremor, says,

AND SOMETIMES HE MUST FIX HIS MISTAKES

Medical
Portraits

Access Check-In

Abecedarian for the Care Shift I Failed to Show Up For

Abandon implies intention, which I must
be honest, is correct in this case: I did
choose not to help you. Wishing I were
dead, or at the very least that I didn't
exist—this depression is both what I felt after
forsaking you and also what kept me from
giving you that ride to the doctor in the first place.
How to compare us: I am plagued by moods I cannot
indoctrinate into the common sense of sense.
Juror of reality I will never be. But your
kidneys do not flush. Every day, those
lithe salts becoming less nimble, losing
momentum, no longer willowing through
nephrons ever-quieter. We both admit to it:
overwhelmed. By my psychosis seeming to limit
possibility instead of expanding. By your blood's
qualifications no longer sufficient, leaving only
redness and stillness. Move, blood. No, I cannot
say that; that was my job. I fucked up. There is
traffic in your tubules. There is a lonely, panicked
urologist. Each of your glomeruli is wrapped in
velvet. My dendritic garden is overrun with
weeds that trap me in my own nonsense, their ugly
xanthophyll making us miss your dialysis appointment.
You cannot tell me it's okay, but you cannot tell me it's not—
there is no right way to end this.

Therapist

She is not very good at her job. Psychosis under control,
we do not get into childhood, the hiding in an empty
dehumidifier box, or going from friend's house
to friend's house, telling each I had eaten at the last.

       Instead, she wants to be my friend, and I think
she could be a good friend if she were not supposed
to be helping me, if she were not some flimsy proxy
for a doctor. But she is. She runs the insurance every week
and I cannot tell what she knows and remembers about me,
whether she is trying to find something bad about me
or has simply run out of meaningful questions.

       I tell her that sometimes when the run
doesn't stretch me enough, I look up the cost of certain
cosmetic procedures. She does not *mmm*, does not ask how
I might find a more innocent way to convene with my stomach
fat. Instead, she asks how much the procedures cost, considers
getting one herself. *No, Angie, shouldn't we just learn to love
our bodies?*

       When I tell her I am trying to get to know
my madness as a friend, she insists that I must start
asking Eli to ensure I take my medication every night.
And sometimes, at home, I hear her voice like I have left
my earbuds on my desk while going to the kitchen and the music
is still playing. The voice says, *You have such a handle on things
it's like you're not even actually ill*, and I wish it were
a hallucination instead of a memory.

       When I want to kill myself
I figure out an approximation of the feeling to share with her
so I am not reinstitutionalized. *I think I would rather be a sunbeam*

than have to exist in this hard and formal body. She gives advice
as if out of a greeting card. *Just because you are in a storm
doesn't mean it is over,* and I know by *it* she means *my life*
but what I hear is *the storm.*

One day, I ask her what she really thinks will happen
when my coverage ends and I must go on living like this.
She says, *To be honest, I think you will probably die from this.*
To her meaning *the sickness.* To me meaning *my life.*

Bench

Eli Invents

new ways of tricking me into taking my antipsychotics every night.

1. We go to Tinuno for kamayan, play puppets with the milkfish
   and squid, and he slips the pills into the shredded mango salad,
   pinches a handful into my mouth.

2. He pretends to get really into cold-pressed juices, turmeric ginger lemon shots
   with cayenne and quetiapine. He tells me that to stomach it
   he needs to hold my hand and take the shot at the same time as me.

3. Folding the pills into American cheese, he insists our dog is too self-conscious
   to take his dewormer alone.

4. The old spoon-as-airplane method, applesauce dripping.

5. After a dazzled night at Crews, a pharmaceutical burlesque: one by one
   undressing the pills from their bottles, svelte fingers placing them
   onto his soft pink tongue, saliva welling, eye contact like a rocket taking off.

   I lie back on the bed propped up on my forearms. He crawls onto me
   slowly, tilts my chin up with one careful thrust of his fingertips
   and kisses me deeply.

Sestina Medicated on 800mg of Antipsychotics

I worry I am faking.
I am doing it for attention.
I want to avoid consequences
so I make people feel bad for me.
Nothing is a reasonable trigger.
I have far too much insight.

It always feels like faking—
I pay too much attention
to a boy and create consequences
for my eagerness. Bad me.
My own mistake is the trigger
and I already have this insight

as the episode starts. Faker.
I pay too much attention
during the episode. The consequence
is self-awareness while the bad me
goes off about being triggered.
It is having this conscious insight

that makes me think I am faking.
I feel that splitting my attention
shouldn't be possible. Consequently,
while I am watching the bad me,
the good me feels triggered
to expose him, in spite

of both being me (sounds fake).
I should just choose to stop, intentionally.
I should just deal with consequences.
I invalidate real schizos—so bad of me.
When an episode is triggered
it should be involuntary, with no insight.

My first psychotic break (fake)
involved hallucinations attending
to me, boys delivering my consequences
for overloving, which was raping me.
Being a bad date shouldn't be a trigger.
It doesn't count. Rob, get inside.

Don't start faking for attention.
There will be consequences. Bad me.
Shit. There is no trigger in sight.

Ward

Window: what allows you to see out
      what separates you from what you see
      your only chance

Ward: to keep away
      to safeguard
      guarded place you are kept

Touched: honored
      possessed
      violated

See someone: a lover
      a therapist
      a hallucination

Murder: crows
      a dying

Institution: me and all my friends
      a dying

Form: a body
      a set of rules
      a set of empty spaces to fill out at the front desk

Derange: to go crazy
      to finally leave a restricted range

Committed: you're staying
you're staying

Chronic: lasting forever
not dead yet

Cavity: an emptiness
a failure to care for yourself like a child
no toothbrush allowed

Hôpital des Beaux Arts

Last week:
a little fit, a raz-
or, a blooming of
tissue. A bit too
far. No more
arms. Up-
on relea-
se from the ER
Venus is enrolled in a part-
ial hospitalization program.
The carpeted rooms, hole-punch
binders, worksheets of acronyms,
circles of plastic chairs like pli-
nths. From an office down the
hall echoes a scream-crying that
must come deep from the belly.
The counselor suggests
squeezing ice next time
she feels the urge. Hand-
less, she resorts to pressing
her bare chest onto the con-
crete floor of the parking gar-
age every morning before group.
She skips breakfast. She does not
feel like eating. She never does any-
more. O case manager, O psychiatric
nurse, O cognitive behavioral thera-
pist—deliver this malformed bosom
unto her discharge plan. Let her
brokenness be revered, her body
made gorgeous by its lack of
reach. Let her pupilless eyes
gaze inward with wonder.

Maid

There is a certain grace in arriving to the apartment this way: the door left unlocked, no rotting body in the living room gnawed by cats who do not understand why no one has fed them in days,[1] the disarray more that of someone gone on vacation than someone too exhausted to avoid disorder.

The maid enters quietly, midafternoon, sent by the hospital as part of the new program.[2] He begins to pick up, uninterested in any sort of mess-based divination, unconcerned with how the sheets got in the bathtub, the dishes under the bed.[3]

He brushes chia seeds from the counter, unplugs the sunlamp left droning at the corner of the desk, innocent. He clears out the bathroom cabinet without checking for the expiration dates on the sertraline and vitamin D and ashwagandha and fish oil.[4] The clothes hang lifeless in the bureau, crisp, unstained, unworn.

Earlier that morning, the complimentary shuttle picked up the apartment's resident, took her to the hospital, the driver unaware of the specifics of her appointment, letting her sit in silence and stare out the window at the world passing lazily by.[5]

---

1   Not that there is a right way to die—only a right to die, hastily disguised
    as the right to live.

2   The maid more accessible than a home. Death more accessible than either.

3   If life is a home that does not come with a maid, is death when the home is finally clean
    or finally empty?

4   I see you trying to keep yourself alive when no one else will I see you
    I see you I see you I see you I promise I see it all

5   There are so many minor finalities, the last opportunity for small talk
    vanishing with each green light driven steadily through—
    not something one might consider missing, and now no time left to miss it.

At the ward, she checks in, the receptionist cheery while clicking checkboxes, printing out one final[6] form to sign. Today the doctor is overbooked, cannot administer the shot, too busy dealing with patients whose suffering[7] requires less creativity.

So a nurse does it, the 3PM procedure, slotted between an appendectomy and a tonsillectomy, the removal of useless bodies[8] once they have succeeded at their uselessness. [NOTE TO SELF: Describe euthanasia scene here once you can bear it.][9]

In the evening, the nurse and the maid both drive home, the city lit up through the windows of offices in vacant skyscrapers. Unknowingly, they pass each other at the stoplight at Medical Drive and Harbor, going in opposite directions,[10] both tired but satisfied[11] at having left the world a cleaner place.[12]

---

6   I think of *terminal* not as in *final* but just as in *a place from which you depart.*
    As in, *I'll see you soon.*

7   How could they be wrong? The masters of their old suffering? Trying to end suffering
    by any means, as if you cannot live in a messy home.
    As if you can't ask me to come over and help clean.

8   If these organs could talk, would they repeat back what we've said about them?
    Can they feel the uselessness inside of them? What is uselessness?

9   Did you get there eventually? Did everything turn out all right?

10 Home in one direction, home in the other: you choose one
    and try not to overshoot.

11 See—it is possible to be both at once, and for this to be okay.

12 Friend, since you left, I've slowly stopped looking for you everywhere. I don't have to—
    you just keep finding me.

Ecologies

Access Check-In

Hardly Creatures

"A healed femur" —anthropologist Margaret Mead, allegedly,
on the first evidence of human civilization

The digital tour guide tells us how we are animals
        as if we don't already know, as if sleep is a game
we play, as if hunger is incidental every day at lunch.
        We enter a virtual room with an improbable flock

of birds suspended at eye level, a hundred
        species flying together. The guide tells us about
a bonded pair of male crows, how when one
        lost his lower mandible to a crashed window

the other began to forage for them both, chewing up
        seeds and worms and pushing the bolus
down his partner's throat. In another room
        we pivot the camera angle and see a hill country creek

running beneath our feet under thick, clear plastic.
        We learn how the blind salamander compensates
for its lack of eyesight with advanced sensitivity
        to changes in water pressure, sweeping its lonely head

back and forth to detect small aquatic invertebrates—
        We creatures have always found a way,
the recording chuckles. We have, I think,
        though this should not mean that we must.

We pause the tour for Rosie to rest with her camera off.
        I wish the guide would stop calling humans creatures, she says.

We're hardly creatures, the way we love each other.
    I nod, but can't stop thinking about the crows

who love each other, the salamander who loves itself,
    the crows who only know caregiving, the salamander
who only knows survival, every creature forever feeding
    whatever mouth is in front of them

either born knowing how to love
    or picking it up down the line.

A Case for Self-Harm

which I cannot write, though I do want to. It does feel good to break. It does
feel better to be broken, for one's outsides to match their insides, the urge

to hurt oneself never truly going away, instead metabolizing into the body,
subsumed into instinct. Inside me, a taut worry presses from beneath

the skin, a mumbled fear twitches like a muscle, a deep-set understanding
itches like a scab: that the tendency to respond to stimuli like this is inborn.

As in: the dog gnaws off its injured leg. The bee delivers its singular sting.
The porcupine never stops pricking itself, stays slicked with fatty antibiotic.

The owl swallows bone and feather in order to eat, reliant on its vomiting,
while the panda simply cannot digest its bamboo. And the blue whale

beaches itself when it knows its time has come, and now we take off
to the museum, stare up at its suspended and incomplete skeleton, and maybe

this moment of awe, this afternoon in which you have dragged me out of bed
will be the best argument: we do not owe health and safety to the world—

but we do. Or at least I do, to you, Eli, and I'm sorry—there is no conclusion
here, and I see my wounded friends, or I don't, but I love them, and I do,

and all these rhythms soon will change, the split arm no longer splitting
toward the truth, the blood sleeping more quietly than we remember,

the grown salmon swimming back into freshwater to spawn.

Bench

Eli Eats Dirt

The boy I love eats dirt. He chews carefully, collects dirt
in jars from different parks, stays stooped over in the dirt
until he is late for his haircut, too focused on grinding dirt
between his teeth. During the day he works his dirty

government job, attempting to keep peace between the dirt
and the democracy. After work, though he is dead tired
he takes no break, ensures a spoonful of each sample is tried.
He creates charts of what his taste can discern in the dirt,

phytoliths indicating how the composition of the dirt
can be traced back to certain ancient plants whose dearth
has left boys like me with minds that reek of dirt.
Some days I do want cure. Someday he will identify dirt

of the correct strain, will spoon it to me while I lie delirious.
Mud will pour from behind my eyes until I am entirely clean.

Nature Poem

I punch myself.
I do it because I want to and I'm an adult now.
I punch myself softly.
I punch myself hard, so hard I remember I am an object.
Every day I punch myself.
I punch myself for fun and I punch myself for work.
I press my cheek against the glass of a skyscraper
and punch the other cheek.
I reach for my keys in my backpack
and punch myself as I reach.
I punch my forearm in Rexall.
I punch my thigh at Loblaws.
At IKEA I hide in the model children's bedroom
and I punch myself in my barely protruding hip bone
with my hand inside a stuffed whale puppet.
I always punch myself discreetly,
alone in my room, or while in public
in such a way that it could be misconstrued
as a mistake.
I never make a mistake.
I know exactly what I am doing.
I go to Yonge-Dundas Square to punch myself.
I cross the diagonal crosswalk there and punch my neck.
I linger by the hip-hop performer and punch my stomach.
I pass the microphones proclaiming
GOD WILL DELIVER YOU
BODY AND SOUL INTO HEAVEN
and I punch that body in the dick.
When I get to heaven I will be bruised

and I will not answer any of God's questions.
What is it called to punch yourself?
What is it called when you are happy?
I punch myself because I like to do it
and it makes me happy.
I want to be happy.
I want to be so, so happy.

History of Display

The history of disabled people in the Western world is in part the history of being on display, of being visually conspicuous while politically and socially erased.
—Rosemarie Garland-Thomson

First dated archaeological record of access
      a complete skeleton except where the left leg should be
      fossilized flowers carefully arranged

The biblical invention of body shame
      (quite foundational really)
then Cain and Abel
then the killing of Abel
      (which I took as a very heavy-handed
      metaphor by God about the creation
      of disabled people but that's just me)

First dated archaeological record of schizophasia
      hieroglyphics whose order suddenly stops making sense
      (see also: first archaeological record of poetry)

Moa categorized as bird even without vestigial wings
Moa goes extinct

Therapeutic Papyrus of Thebes (not great)
St. Mary of Bethlehem (Bedlam) (not great)
Various other specialized schools/hospitals/asyla (often indiscernible)
"Idiocy" "Imbecility" "Lunacy" "Insanity" "Feeble-mindedness" (not great)

Autism evolves as next logical human progression
        (powerful thought specialization,
        less time wasted on trivial concerns
        e.g. social conventions, verbal tact)

The schizophrenias evolve
as a means of good vibes

Mad people exist in public
        (guys this one doesn't go well)
Mad people existing in public deemed a failure of the state
        mad people not considered part of the public
        mad people considered the part of the public that is scary
        mad people denied private housing
(Not sure where to put this in timeline; kind of an "always" thing?)

Electroconvulsive therapy
Lobotomy
Forced sterilization
A bunch of other stuff (bad) (let's not get into it)
Coffee cold-brewed
Bottomless brunch w/ Aperol Spritzes

Eloquence invented
(working on getting rid of this one ASAP)

As a child at summer camp I am told
bananas have a vitamin that makes you happy
        I eat bananas until I am sick and vomit
        think: *this must be happiness*

First person to step out to the bathroom
       while at a party and have a little freak-out moment
       while their exasperated reflection sighs at them

Carcinization discovered
All crab-looking creatures continue to be called crabs

Theater built inside CAMH (?)
Graveyard built off-site
for Austin State Hospital (?!)

Lana Del Rey releases *Born to Die*
       causing thousands of adolescents
       to develop clinical depression

My junior year of high school
       temporary mania-induced hyperthymesia (idk how)
My sophomore year of college
       develop schizoaffective disorder bipolar type
       which all my high-school friends say in hindsight
       we totally could have seen coming

Why am I like this first uttered with disgust

My new meds make me sooooo sleepy
       this does not fade ever

My first seven boyfriends make my psychosis worse
       (this isn't necessarily a bad thing
       because I do usually love my psychosis
       but in these seven situations
       it did end up being really bad oops lol)

First and only time I wake up early
        to see the sunrise over the lake
        so now I can sleep through it forever

Horaglanis populi discovered
        blind catfish that lives in the subterranean pores
        of aquifers (its whole life!) (yes it has a whole life!)

God stops showing up to creation meetings
        (very overwhelmed and trouble
        with insurance covering his psychotherapy)
God forgets to refill his prescription
God forgets to cool down the earth
God forgets to reinvent homeostasis
Wendy Williams performs "Native New Yorker"

First gay porn with disabled Asian top
First successful barista friendship in new country
Eli finishes community-center course on caretaking
Arrival of the countertop mini-dishwasher (game changer)

Why am I like this first mumbled with wonder

Vilazodone goes generic
The nurse practitioner hugs me on his last day
First time my mom calls me *disabled* of her own accord

Final time I show up to the intramural fields
        in the middle of the night
        and the sprinklers turn on
        and I shout *I'm here! I'm real!*

        This field is real and I'm here
        in this field and I'm real!

Audiovisual Room

Access Check-In

Short Film

At Tangled

We are about to host our first in-person event at the gallery
in three years. Sarah, Clay, and I spend two hours trying
the owl-shaped camera that will track whoever is the speaker
and spotlight them on the synchronous livestream event.
Rumi and Jessie are over in the corner of the office figuring out
what food to order. After a bit, they settle on sushi.

But I'm vegan, Alex has a feeding tube, Kevin can't lift sushi,
Graham is severely allergic to soy (can't even be in the gallery),
and then we need a side of fries just in case Leah comes out
since she has ARFID—it's all possible, just takes a bit of trying.
Then, when we are pre-screening the films before the event,
we realize we need content warnings. I lean against the big speaker

noting the timestamps of the triggers, the moments when the speaker
in the film swears loudly, and I imagine I am blissfully eating sushi
so I don't get triggered myself. Soon people arrive, the event
talk begins, everyone in chairs or flopped onto cushions on the gallery
floor. Lorraine shows up and says anybody who wants can try on
the leopard-print masks that she keeps in a bag that hangs out

on the back of her powerchair. Then the films start and right out
of the gate it's naked bodies and hospital echoes, the ASL speakers
and low-vision folks alike gasping at the images and audio, trying

to follow the intricate plot, and then the food arrives late, the sushi
on crip time, and Rumi and Jessie set it up in the back of the gallery.
I'm playing access doula, monitoring the chat on the Zoom event

which blows up when the doctor transplants the heart. Eventually
the film ends. Everybody applauds in ASL so the sensory out-
put doesn't overwhelm, then shuffles to the back of the gallery
for food. *You know if the transplanted organ fails*—Helen speaks
to me earnestly, wonder in her voice—*the patient can sue.* She
widens her eyes. *Sue who? The dead donor? Go try it!*

We go on, discuss transplantation's moral implications, trying
out theories until the guests and interpreters have left the event.
We ordered too much, so I claim an untouched tray of sushi
as I say bye. Dan and I walk toward home together, hashing out
the new moon's astrological impact. We never really speak
much at work, but now we're laughing, even outside the gallery

after the event. Before we part, he turns to me, balancing sushi:
Hey, let me know if you ever need anything, okay? I'm trying out
having needs now, my gallery filled with beloved guest speakers.

Artist Talk

Actually, I don't want to do this anymore. Can we stop?

Agh. Okay, okay. Thanks. Thank you.

I'm going to go now.

Hands flipped from up with scrunched fingers
to down and flat with furrowed eyebrows.

Fists lowered and opened with raised eyebrows.

Grimace. Nod. Flat hand tapped on chin then moved forward and down.

Point toward self. Hand pulled away from temple while closing fingers.
Hands moved down with wrists up and pinky and thumb extended.

Bench

Eli Plays Along

I. Phone Call

Hey, where are you? Hey, breathe, it's okay, I'm not upset. No, I'm not trying to make you come home, I just felt like hanging out with my boyfriend! Where are you, I could come and—oh, wow, really? That sounds really unfair of him to make you do that. And so that is the reason you left, to find him? No, I'm not mad at him. No, I wouldn't let him hurt me, it's okay for you to tell me. Here, why don't I come help you find him, and I can bring a flashlight. Yes, I'd love to sing with you, that's very smart since you know it will keep you safe. I'll even bring the cards and some Sprite Zero and after we find him we can all have a picnic together, I bet he'll like that. Yes, we can take the train home instead of a car, I know you love a night train. No, I'd never be mad, I love you when you're like this. After nights like these you twitch in your sleep which means I get lots of extra squeezes, it's my favorite. Where are you, angel? Take your time. Take your time, angel. Oh, great, this will be so fun, I've never been to that park at this time of night! I bet the floodlights are beautiful. Are they beautiful? Tell me what floodlights you can see, beautiful.

II. CART Transcription

Haywire art you. Day brief—it's ok. Hymn ought up, sad no. Hymn ought dry into my achy. Oh, come home. Eye just fell, the light hanging, outwit my poise. Friend, wear art. You, I, good command. Awhile reeling—that sound. Real lean fare, a vim, tum ache, yuzu, that. Dance soda, dizz the reeds in. You lift to find dim. No whim not made. At hymnal, eye wooden to lit hymn, herd meet. Soak A for you too. Till me, hear wide own tie. Cum hell pew fine. Dim in dye can. Preen, guff-laugh, slight yeah. Side love, two seeing width youth adds fairies. Mart sins, you no wit; whelk heap you save. Aisle eve in burying thick hearts. Handsome spry tizz hero, handoff tear. Wi-Fi and dim, weekend awl half. A pick, neck to gather. I bet hell like that. Yes weekend ache, the train omen steady fucker. I know you'll. Often height rain. Know widen. Ever be. Mad I love you. Win. You're like this. Have tern heights, slight these. You to wish inner sleep, wish mean sigh get. Lots of fix, trust queasies. Sits my fake veer. It wear—are you? Wane jeweled. Ache your time. Day cure time. Angel. O gray to thistle bees, O fun ivy. Never be in-tooth, at perk, at distime. Of night, I bed. The flood. Lie to sore be you. Too full, are they be you? Too full · till me. What flood! Lights you can see! Be you. Too full.

Hopescrolling

The addiction not to my phone but to the people inside my phone. To be able to open community at will. To close it at will. To be together while alone. To share something, anything, with the world, with the distance hurtling closed.

A brown professor tweets about a brown student who quickly solved a linguistic puzzle in a novel. The replies praise her comprehension of purposefully unclear language. The other replies question this praise.

A shorebird catches a butterfly and dips it in river water before swallowing / *she's a sauce girl I have to respect it / like a birria taco i'm crying*

A young Black girl: *We're all deaf, hands were being thrown, we're all signing arguing over some boy, then suddenly it was dark—the girl who was hosting the sleepover cut the lights. It was dead silent, literally. I couldn't even be mad at her, 'cause like damn, she really got me there.*

A straight Black man: *Really in the mood to have a bad day!* 42.7k likes, 10.6k retweets

Two white girls with vocal fry talk about loving their mental illnesses. The video is removed the next day and the podcast goes on hiatus. Buried in the hate comments of their other videos: *Wait, but they were kinda right . . .*

A sighted user uses the alt text of an image to hide spoilers for an episode of *Survivor*. A blind user responds spoiling the rest of the season.

A livestream of a car driving down a dark and endless road. In the comments sections, a steady flow of users posting their secrets. Mixed in: *Thank you*. Mixed in: *We won't tell.*

A tweet from Dr. Roberta Bobby: *Hi diva . . . can I call you diva? My name is Detective Fierce . . . You're not in trouble boots, we're just trying to get the tea on this situation . . .* Eli will repeat this for months. Literally nonstop for months.

The gym routine of a straight, white, male wheelchair user who does pull-ups with his chair. Everyone in the comments desperately wants to fuck him.

A white woman shouts that someone at the back of her plane is not real. For weeks after, the clip circulates. I eventually hunt down a post that includes her name and response.

A disco ball hangs from the IV drip of a teenager with gastroparesis. *I eat through my heart and I'm absolutely thriving!*

Drag Race Philippines plays in the background while a bakla putters around making dinner. He does not know the language, he does not read the subtitles, but still somehow he knows to sit exactly when the queens start dancing.

A queer Black femme with ME/CFS shares a day in her life unable to leave the apartment. From bed she vogues, practicing hand counts. *Just imagine I have legs for days.*

lowkey life hack if ur mentally ill just become too busy to experience the symptoms bc i've had this raging urge for a Girl Interrupted moment and quite frankly haven't had the fucking time

A brown man with a limp flops over the turnstile with his cane, limps to the emergency exit, opens it for a stranger in a wheelchair, a stranger with a guide dog.

The camera is pointed down at the subway passenger's feet. We hear another passenger sustain a scream for over thirty seconds. Huge mood.

The girlfriend slides along the sling above her partner who is in his chair. Audio from a different video plays: *I feel like you're just here for the zipline.*

With over 100 allergies, she buys a kitchen appliance to turn her glucose supplement into sorbet, tastes dessert for the first time in years.

Very genuine alt text in the reaction image: *Someone in an Elmo costume walking along a city street, but Elmo looks deflated and weird, is wearing a crossbody bag and appears to have either snow or cocaine all over his head.*

Each of their branded gay white husband prank videos begins with *My husband is blind :D* When he is rejected for a treatment, they cry, say *We will get through this together.*

In the shaky Eras Tour livestream, the first notes of "right where you left me" crackle through. Fans comment the lyrics so quickly that there is no need for live captioning.

I forgot to charge my ears last night. He shows us his six rechargeable batteries, rushes to work. *I put 'em on even though I knew they were dead. Just a gesture.*

Best friends trying on wedding dresses reach to slow-dance together, one remembering too late that the other has no arm there.

On the first day of summer, a parakeet pecks out on a soundboard: *I – WANT – FEEL – SAD*

Pretty privilege strikes again, she smirks, describing how a man at Taco Bell asked if she needed any sauces. *Then I remembered—I've just got one hand.*

A gay brown Deaf man presses his cheek to the pulsing club wall, puts the phone in his mouth while Grindr notifications go off, hears the rush with his bones.

sorry bro cant go out tongiht forgot to charge my leg. He shows us how to charge it, tells us not to forget, *or don't lose your leg, that would probably be beneficial as well.*

Grimace posts a selfie, writes his own alt text. *A picture of me (Grimace) being happy and waving goodbye with my right hand. I am wearing very cool shades. There's a red umbrella behind me with a McDonald's logo. Hamburglar and Birdie are standing next to me but we can barely see them as i do not know how to crop a picture properly*

An article reports that the Los Angeles Dodgers have quietly re-signed a schizophrenic player for a fifth year so he will not lose his health insurance despite no longer playing. *Sadly, Toles is just a shadow of his former self.* There is no report yet on his new self.

He replaces all the lights in his house with 100W bulbs before his low-vision lover comes over for their second date.

Laughter, somehow.
Laughter, everywhere.

Sensory
Room II

Access Check-In

Access Rider

To shower in the dark.
To waste time speaking.
To stutter my hands.
To ask for help.

To ignore the help offered.
To cry into coffee.
To microwave a tortilla.
To call this my prime.

To not be so brave.
To stay on the phone.
To follow me home.
To not leave myself.

Access Request

If I told you what was happening I would be breaking the rules.

If I articulated the feeling it would violate the protections.

We have placed the protections around the articulation of feelings.

Everything I believe about my own preexisting condition is a superstition.

Superstition is the kindest way I have found to describe delusion.

Every avoidance of my condition is a delusion surrounding delusion.

A superstition surrounding superstition is an overthinking.

I will be fine. I am overreacting.

One cannot think their way out of a thinking disorder.

It does not help to create a list of the horrors.

The list of horrors is a list of ways I have found to render success.

If I told you what was happening I would be successful.

What is happening is wrong, which I have found is a way to live.

Everything is wrong. I feel like myself right now.

Three Translations of an Email to My Boss

Easy Read

Dear Heather,

I sincerely regret the necessity of composing this email, the basis of which I understand presents inequitable consequences for the foremost commitment we maintain to our mission of collective care, interdisciplinary development, and critical ideation-action processes. Unfortunately, today I have encountered a number of individualized dilemmas related to my socio-medical temperament which have severely imposed on my capacity to conduct business affairs at an adequate level to contribute meaningfully to our present endeavors. It is my intention to administer an internal audit, follow up swiftly with the pertinent treatments required to restore my condition, and reinstitute a more attuned and masterful presentation of my character for our next strategic planning session. Please accept my profound apologies; I look forward with genuine eagerness to returning to our collaboration together posthaste.

Regards,
Robert M. Colgate

Hi Heather,

Sorry, this sucks, and I feel bad missing things bc our project rn is legitimately rly cool and important. Anyway I had an episode last night, don't have to get into it, I'm fine and handling it, but I can't get anything done today ugh. Gonna take a minute to rest, get some help, and should be fine for meeting tomorrow. Seriously so sorry, thanks for bearing with me, can't wait to get back at it when I'm better.

Thanks,
Rob

Heathereatherer

sorry sorry the good thing and us are good things and things and good and yes
we have to have have to and help yes Rob not so Rob but is Rob and will Rob
just is being right now is so being is soooo being not being though yes up and
take haha take and time will less time and more Rob ok gonna move and be
and go to under where Rob is Rob not Rob but Rob that under strange under

Thanks thanks best best
me

omfg

oh my fkn god i am so sick of this i literally can't do this anymore i don't want to
be articulate i don't care about "rendering arresting images" idk why i decided
this would be the way i talk about being a little schizo faggot freak like i'm fucking
exhausted of convincing you that we are happy to be alive jesus christtttt i don't
want to fight for us anymore i just want to sleep for a thousand fucking years
if i have to come up with one more metaphor to make our exceptionalit–
exceptionalnes– whatEVER oh myy godddd, our being exceptional
more apparent to you, if i, uh, have to—what was i saying—uh,
uh. fuck. god i'm tired. here's the thing: i don't need us to have
matching wounds i just need you to know what a wound is.
why am i wounding myself to do that why am i doing all
this for ableds who already have everything jfc crips
deserve frivolity we deserve ease and rest why am i
reaching into this deep well of unwellness just to
prove that when i don't even think you want to
listen like do you even like poems or are you
just reading this at some coffee shop to
seem cultured omfg these poems will
not make you into a better person
idk what i have to give to you
omfg idk what i even have
what do you mean i have
to give out hope what
are you even talking
about hope hope
where am i
supposed
to get
hope

I Need a Minute

Slow down. No poem on this page.

Fine Art

Access Check-In

God Is in the Gallery

doing a performance piece.

He and a madwoman sit opposite each other in hardback chairs
staring at each other from across the empty room.

God says, *I will show you how you needn't suffer for my name.*

Immediately, something like scales fall from her temples
and she perceives the room with great precision.

The audience erupts into applause
until they realize the woman is shrieking.

Put them back.

Self-Portrait and Tactile Replica as Living Ghost

I. *Original Work (Please do not touch.)*

Throughout the gallery, ghosts, of all senses:
ordinary invisible ghosts that no one can see

except the blind, ghosts in the audio room that only
the deaf can hear, ghosts in the thresholds felt only

by phantom limbs, ghosts hanging around like paintings
suspended too high to be experienced as intended by anyone

sitting, only discernible to those floating above their own
bodies as if dissociating in front of the Monkmans.

Each ghost born from that part of a person that dies
when, creeping through the museum on any Tuesday,

slowly, frame by frame, you find there is no art for you.
No portraits of haunting resemblance, no shared institutions

on the didactic panels, no synonymy of color or shape
or function—just the realization that everything beautiful

ever created for you was the result of an explicit request,
and now on the subway home it is harder to believe

that the boy actually wants to hold your hand, that you
are not simply part of a quietly funded diversity initiative

whose sponsor is very satisfied, very proud of himself,
putting up with your moods as you stare slack-jawed

at your reflection in the subway window and understand:
this is the only portrait of yourself that you get. And now

the train arrives at the next stop, your reflection disappears
in the station's cruel light, you are not home yet,

and now over the loudspeakers comes crackling
the city's insistent refrain:

Please stand clear of the closing doors.
Please do not make this harder on everyone.

11. *Tactile Replica (Feel free to touch this version of the art.)*

me

my

hand

  now

                              me

        now   me

Please
Please

On Sex

Tallies in marker on the small of the back
No

These contortions as the source of our deepest oppression
No

His fingers a needle skipping across your bent record
Yes

The legalities of disclosing status
Maybe

Seroconversion into madness like a virus
No

Seduction with madness like a charisma
Sure

Socks that grip the ground like the anus grips the penis
No

Stares as you stumble down Queen at 1AM talking to yourself
Nah

Stares as you catwalk down Queen at 1AM looking fuckable
Yas

Removing the body to be left with the self
Please

Knowing exactly what you are doing
No

Knowing the exact angle the semen will come out
No

Museum with no art in it
The body

Museum of unreasonable pain
The body

Museum of the body
The mind

Empty Frame for the Artist Who Was Too Sick to Ever Finish the Work or Make It to the Gallery

Bench

Eli Interprets

At the Kim Petras concert I watch the sign-language interpreter during
    "Throat Goat."

These lips go la la la / Give me that ya ya ya ya

Curved hands rotating above each other in opposite directions
just below the mouth. Cheeks sucked in then puffed out.

How silly, to understand anything.

On my way home, I feel the familiar click
of my tongue falling down my throat.

I walk into the apartment hitting my head with a teaspoon.
When we get on FaceTime, Eli is chopping scallions,
glancing over at the phone. He asks how I am. I attempt:

*It's always dark and start and go and go and there's no Rob
that is awake it's always dark and sleep and goodbye and please.*

He nods. *Yes, dark, you. Personally, I'd be happy if you stayed alive.*

I walk circles around my studio, a procrastinating ghost.
Eli asks whether I've had anything to eat. I try again:

If there were no laws laws not—   *I think absent circles—*
Illegal circles if I existed worse—   *Rob illegal circles and want if—*

My nonsense interrupts itself, it does not correspond.

Still, Eli nods. *Ah, you want sushi. You're a bit schizo*
and want to break your veganism to get a salmon roll.

The bodega worker is used to this by now.
As I check out, he waves hello to the tiny Eli in my phone.

In the morning, my voice apologizes to Eli while I lag behind.
I'm so lucky, he replies. *I get to hear four brilliant ways you'd start every sentence.*
Anyway, I saw a new bird yesterday, I heard this strange call in the park . . .

While I listen, I decide I cannot die. Not yet.
He has so many more songs to figure out.

The Body Is Not an Apology
Except for Mine Sometimes

I have a reputation for being loved but not in a good way
like how a corporate worker loves their office. I am an office
and the cubicles pattern on endlessly, each quiet and empty
yet not quite fit for sleep. In every city I have lived in
I have many memories but they are all of me falling asleep
on different unremarkable nights, thinking the same thoughts
every time—*I don't know how to do this, I don't know why I have to.*
I am not brilliant. I do not know how flowers work.
I do not pay for the bus. I save my token so that I might
have an excuse for the heaviness that slows me. There is weight
I want to sanctify and there are people I want to forget.
There are people I want to remember and when they call
still I wonder: *why.* When the crow dies the vultures must eat it.
When disability dies I must bring it back from the dead
so I can keep being myself. When gender dies I must find a way
to remain fabulous. One thing about psychosis is that the physics
are fabulous. This is perhaps a problem. I should learn more
about problems. Let the sickness fill me so I might live full.
Let the brain remain swollen to close up memory's gaps.
In the distance I saw dancing. In the distance I saw no more distance.

The Friending of Burden

Suffering: as in, something to care about. As in, still alive, the extending of certain
survival, how we elaborate *suffered and died* to indicate the ending of burden.

All this shame in pursuing happiness, in abandoning sadness with no one
to care for it—I understand this sounds like the defending of burden.

When you are drowning, a short breath is better than none. But when
you are crazy, any flash of clarity forces a contending with burden.

I grab the boy by the shoulders, shake him, scream at him to pull himself
together, throw a drink in his face—it's me, bartending my burden.

I'm Rob? I've been Rob this whole time? Thank god for psychosis so I don't
have to believe any of this actually happened, the sublime suspending of burden.

On the wall I am the painting, my body the security guard standing in front,
but he is on his phone, having long lost interest in attending to burden.

I begin to miss the thrill of volatility, obsession, incessance. When health
comes to me, dull and bored, I find myself recommending him burden.

Why this fear still? There is always a theater in the hospital where we dance.
There is always a makeshift school where we learn by comprehending our burden.

I have fallen in love with what I cannot do. To have a limit: how delightfully human.
A relief, to lack the responsibility of a god to solve that which impendingly burdens.

Me and Rosie complaining office stories—this is where I catch us laughing.
Those nights scrubbing Colgate into her teeth, joyful in the codepending of burden.

Self-Portrait Without Sense of Self

During a routine pass through New York City, I attend my requisite hang-out with the friend who saved my life in college. She doesn't care about me anymore, and she shouldn't. We sit in the back of a gay bar, the wallpaper tessellations of men penetrating each other, and I watch her stare past me.

I stare past my laptop at the reflection of the sunset fading in the adjacent skyscraper. Eli comes home to me sitting in the near dark. *You like it better this way, don't you?* I don't know how to agree. I don't know how to tell him that I am the sunset but my body is the red reflection. That he is stuck being the sky.

The Red River Cultural District becomes accessible by virtue of me having an episode there. Tuezgayz at Barbarella becomes a hospital by virtue of Gabbie and Eli taking care of me there. I don't like me. I put down my tequila sunrise, watch one hand reach toward the dance floor. I watch my other hand grab it and pull back.

Pulling on my backpack after another skyscraper appointment, I cannot help but to still suspect dysfunction, hidden beneath the purposed necessity of a larger cure. I lie on the elevator floor. At home, the bottoms of all my mugs grow stained with myo-inositol powder, little white angels I do not trust but drink anyway as a gesture toward survival.

In a gesture toward survival, I decide I should tell my mother of the doctor's refusal. I want her to say, *Why is he punishing your body to cure your mind?* Instead she says, *Well, he was probably right not to trust you, don't you think?*

No thinking while I am in the shower, just wet and noise and drain. A fitness influencer's TikTok loops endlessly from where I've left my phone by the sink: *You just have to listen to your body instead of punishing it.* Under the dribble of water, I listen to my body, then spit back at it: *I don't believe you.*

I don't believe I belong at the conference in Lisbon. Every morning, I put on Eli's clothes first, then my own clothes over them. All day I am aware of the slight discomfort, the snag of my belt loops. Eating salt shrimp with Banu, I say, *I feel nostalgic for the life I'm living right now.* She says, *I think that means you're happy.* I say, *I think it means I'm sad.*

At Sad Girl Sundays, I watch the two very average, very white twinks start making out at the drop of Lady Gaga's "Rain on Me," both unaware of my staring. I spend another nine dollars on a vodka soda but dream of calamansi. When I walk into the lobby of the apartment building, Kevin and the coffee table quickly stop laughing and glance at me.

I glance at the selfie I have just taken, think, *No.* I stare at it, think, *No.* I come back to it later, think, *If only I looked like that.*

If only I looked better today, I think to myself at drag brunch, looking out at the sea of pale torsos in crop tops. Between lipsyncs, I tell Kevin that I am trying to learn to speak, less as a way of speaking and more as a way of proving that I exist. *Isn't it all just noise,* he offhands, staring at a man. The city hall bell tower clangs, the chimes random, counting no hour, making no sense.

Nonsense, I'm sorry for avoiding you at the party. When I moved to this city, I told myself I would go off-book, tell people about us. But still the pharmacist knows my name, says hi when I am only stopping in for chips. Still I function high without believing in it. I wake early, I hustle—forgive me this function.

Functionally, it's free accommodaysh, I text Eli as I consider institutionalizing myself. No paying rent or buying groceries, free time to read, never forgetting to stop by the pharmacy. When we say someone has gone crazy, we must first ask why they wanted to go.

Don't go, disorder. I remember when you used to be a sign of joy—Eli's kitchen after a dinner party, or the canvas tote of groceries left spilling onto on the counter in the rush to get into bed, socks still on. You were not just this fear that I carry, a plastic bag cutting into my palm which I must not go home without.

I go home without groceries often. At 10:30PM I force myself to go to Wheatsville, creep through the health-food aisle, unable to afford the right shape of konjac root that will convince me that I should be alive. So I palm the peaches. I thump the melons. I am thumping the melons. I am thumping the melons to keep from killing myself.

To keep from killing myself, I trek to a Filipino art show at a suburban community center. A still life painting of peach-flavored glucose tablets in a fruit bowl. A plaster cast of a bottle of metformin. A quilt stitched out of used compressions socks. None of the artists are charging more than $100 for their work. There is only one bench. One bench is enough.

Enough, Rob. Then, *I'm sorry, I can't stop, I can't breathe.* Then, *This is one of those things you need to be able to say you've been through.* The cursor shakes uncontrollably as I move it toward the Zoom link.

The subway zooming under Yonge, I read Tim Dlugos, listen to Chappell Roan—but I am not doing that. I am watching myself do that from above, impressed with my falseness, how I imitate a life. I have begun to count on things fading: the sound of the music as the lyrics empty into you, everything you remember from that one book, the train in its tunnel, that self-loathing feeling, the sun.

The sun is insane to never miss a morning. From the abandoned lifeguard chair, I stare directly at it. I must trust that light is good. Still, I am scared of the days, though they are the sole container of everything I love.

Empty containers of brown rice, coarse-ground coffee, frozen berries, everything I try to love. I clean the kitchen in silence, gaze at myself in the dead glass of the induction burner, the dry skin and cracked eyes of a young cartographer convincing himself: *someday someone will need these maps.*

Maps I never use spill out of the glove compartment when the boy kneeling in front of me in the footwell knocks it open. Later, at the lake, I sit in my sweat, alone on the big rocks, wondering whether I have chosen wrong, trying to have a moment, but I get distracted by my phone, and then it gets dark, and then it's all over.

Community Records

Access Check-In

Abecedarian After Forgetting
Yesterday's Medication

Up on Shaw, deep winter, after teaching at the school for
madpeople, my students and I ride the street-
car together—not necessarily home, just away, through
blizzards that always arrive after our night classes. One night,
Kathy, collector of strange vintage dolls, asks Lily what her
nalgene is full of. *Skim milk. I have to drink fourteen liters of*
fluid every day. Damn lithium. I nod, remark that I used to
take lamotrigine but ended up getting the potentially fatal
xerosis side effect all over my arms. *So now I be on that*
Zepidone grind, I blab. Lily squeals, deems us diagnosis
sisters, schizoaffective and bipolar close enough. Inevitably
our chatter jumps about, turns to 24/7 cafés for late-night writing.
You can't forget—these are circadian rhythm disorders, she says.
It's true. I recall junior year, when I'd jog instead of sleep, and
Lily laughs. *But it does make certain things easier.* We list:
raves, red-eyes, midnight premieres and album drops. *Plus,*
just saying, I can get all my work done in the same hours of the same
day that sanies get. It just takes some time-bending, some reordering
expectation. Months later, summer like a broth steaming our
humid city, I take the streetcar up Spadina to grab
pho with her. We wander through the same conversations as
all those storms ago, damp and restless aboard the sluggish 501
Queen: still up all night, still weighed down by salts,
verses still running through our minds like streetcars.
Gotta be a strange place to run through. Lily grins, shoots me a
wink, assures me it is a wink and not a lithium twitch.

Seafood City

My mother, craving familiarity, drives
to Seafood City. She pushes the cart,

scanning the shelves, casually steering past
old married couples, tired mothers with children,

college roommates collecting their weekly haul
of noodles and eggs for palabok—she is here

to listen to them talk, not eavesdropping
as much as just letting Tagalog wash over her,

unexceptional conversations about shrimp and rice
and diabetes and home. In my neighborhood

I don't know anyone else whose native language
is schizophasia. But I, too, want a city made

of seafood. I want to bump into my neighbors
in the elevator with no fear of my drowned tongue.

I want to invite them over for word salad, to mix
our chatter into halo-halo for dessert. When I confess

Sorry, I forgot my mouth today, wringing my clammy hands,
I want them to smile, reply, *That's totally fine, I forgot my ears.*

The Softness of Language

Rob

I will have Eli wake me up from my self-sedated sleep. I will get dressed in clothes that Eli washed fresh for my long day. I will wear that softest blouse and skinniest khakis that Eli steamed. I will grab the lunch he made me and head out into this city that knows me only as collateral damage. After I get to Lorraine's, I will lift her myalgic body out of bed into her chair, put on her myrtle dress, and make her the softest eggs, slowly melting cheese, watching the spinach shrink like one in their exhaustion wishes the day would, though it doesn't.

She will roll and I will walk to campus. She will wait for me while I push yet another button, unexceptionally, for the thousandth time: elevator, door, door, elevator, elevator, door, vending machine, door, toilet, sink, door, laptop, broadband projector. I will leave and she will encourage her myriad students, will teach them to be soft and stimmy in class.

After class she will roll and I will walk to the park together and talk about feeling alone. I will tell her how I am thinking of disowning language, though technically nothing is wrong with my life. The calm is not astonishing anymore. We are used to living this way, disinterested, undefined, snacking on fruit I place in our mouths, the figs soft and thankful to the many wasps whose deaths are their definition.

Lorraine

I will ▮▮▮ wake ▮ up ▮▮ my self ▮▮▮▮▮ will ▮▮▮▮▮▮▮ ▮▮▮▮▮ wash ▮ fresh ▮▮ my ▮▮▮▮▮▮▮▮▮▮ soft ▮▮▮▮ ▮ skin ▮▮▮▮▮ that ▮ i steam ▮ I will grab ▮ lunch ▮▮▮▮ ▮ out in ▮ this city ▮▮▮▮▮▮▮▮ later ▮▮ After ▮▮▮ I ▮ lift ▮ my ▮ body out of bed ▮▮▮▮▮ put on ▮ my ▮ dress and make ▮▮▮ soft ▮ eggs ▮▮▮ melt ▮ cheese watch ▮ spinach shrink like ▮▮▮▮ exhaustion ▮▮▮▮▮▮▮▮▮ doesn't.

▮▮▮▮▮▮ I will walk to campus ▮ will ▮▮▮▮▮▮ push ▮ no ▮ button ▮ except ▮▮ for the ▮▮▮▮▮▮ ▮▮▮▮▮▮▮▮ vending machine ▮▮▮▮▮▮ laptop ▮▮▮ and projector. I ▮▮▮▮▮ will encourage ▮ my ▮ students, will teach ▮▮▮▮▮▮▮ my ▮ class.

After class ▮▮▮▮ I will walk to the park ▮▮▮▮▮▮ ▮ alone. ▮▮▮▮ I ▮▮▮ own ▮ language ▮ ▮▮▮▮▮▮▮▮ my life ▮▮▮▮▮▮▮▮▮▮▮ ▮ more ▮▮▮▮▮▮▮ defined ▮▮▮ ▮▮▮▮▮▮▮ than ▮▮▮ any ▮ ▮▮▮▮▮ definition.

Rob & Lorraine

wash our language fresh
each I more than I—a team
soft definitions

Bench

Eli's App History, February 4–5, Messages Accidentally Erased

Saturday, February 4

10:04AM ET—DoorDash
 KUPFERT & KIM @ 140 Spadina Ave, Toronto, ON M5V 2L4
 Açai Smoothie, K&K Waffle (GF), Iced Matcha Latte (Soy)
 Delivery to Rob Colgate @ BrightHomes Condo, Toronto, ON M5V 2Z1
  Add note to gift receipt: "i love you chickadee :3"

12:14PM ET—Google Maps
 "stanley park vancouver parking lot"
 "brunch near stanley park vancouver"

1:57PM ET—Apple Pay
 SIEGAL'&;S BAGELS $13.38
 JJ BEAN COFF ROAS $5.59

2:20PM ET—ParkMobile
 ZONE 2178 3:00HR EXP 5:20PM PAYBYCARD

4:49PM ET—Photos
 STORAGE ALERT: 0.13GB storage remaining
 226 new photos added

6:02PM ET—iNaturalist
 226 new observations uploaded
 3 first-time species observations
  Red-Breasted Sapsucker, Willow Flycatcher, Black-Headed Grosbeak

6:30PM ET—WOWPresents+
   Drag Race Brasil, Season 1, Episode 1: What's Up, Lindas!
   Drag Race Brasil, Season 1, Episode 2: Frenemies
   Drag Race Brasil, Season 1, Episode 3: Tupiniquees

6:52PM ET—Kayak
   Roundtrip YVR <> RIO

9:12PM ET—FaceTime
   INCOMING: Rob Colgate (16 minutes, 8 seconds)

9:14PM ET—Google
   "open wine no corkscrew"
   "fun drinking games"

9:19PM ET—Spotify
   SharePlay: Squidward Nose • cupcakKe • 3:09

9:26PM ET—Contacts
   FIRST NAME: Sarah LAST NAME: Toronto COMPANY: Rob Friend
   FIRST NAME: Helen LAST NAME: Toronto COMPANY: Rob Friend

9:28PM ET—Google
   "woody's & sailor toronto drag bar"
   "georgie girl instagram"
   "sofonda cox instagram"
   "long distance partner social life"
   "comparing self to partner"
   "queer birding meet up vancouver"

9:45PM ET—TikTok

Sunday, February 5

12:32AM ET—Find My Friends
  Rob Colgate

12:38AM ET—Find My Friends
  Rob Colgate

12:39AM ET—Google Maps
  "woody's & sailor toronto"

12:45AM ET—Phone
  OUTGOING: Rob Colgate (voicemail)

12:48AM ET—Find My Friends
  Rob Colgate

12:49AM ET—Phone
  OUTGOING: Rob Colgate (voicemail)
  OUTGOING: Rob Colgate (voicemail)
  OUTGOING: Rob Colgate (voicemail)
  OUTGOING: Sarah Toronto (voicemail)
  OUTGOING: Helen Toronto (voicemail)

12:52AM ET—Google
  "seroquel and alcohol"
  "seroquel half life"
  "iphone dead or no service"
  "track no service iphone"

12:55AM ET—Find My Friends
  Rob Colgate

12:56AM ET—Phone

    INCOMING: Helen Toronto (0 minutes, 56 seconds)

    OUTGOING: Rob Colgate (voicemail)

    OUTGOING: Rob Colgate (voicemail)

    OUTGOING: Rosie Toronto (4 minutes, 27 seconds)

1:02AM ET—Find My Friends

    Rosie Toronto wants to share location with you. ACCEPT?

    Rob Colgate

1:08AM ET—Phone

    INCOMING: Rosie Toronto (1 hour, 55 minutes)

3:03AM ET—FaceTime

    INCOMING: Rob Colgate (10 hours, 28 minutes)

3:08AM ET—Lyft

    ALERT: Your pickup seems far from your current location. Still want to book?

    Trip: Feb 5, 2023 • 3:08am • 6.2km • 16 minutes

    PICKUP: 3:08am, Christie Pits Park, Toronto, ON M6G 3K4

    DROP-OFF: 3:24am, BrightHomes Condo, Toronto, ON M5V 2Z1

1:31PM ET—Instacart

    REXALL, 250 University Ave Unit #120, Toronto, ON M5H 3EH

        Liquid IV™ Hydration Multiplier (12 sachets)

        Tylenol™—Extra Strength 500mg Caplets (24 ct)

        3.25" Mini Love Ya So Much Love Card

        Ezy Dose™ 7-Day AM/PM Pill Reminder

    MINISO, 219 Queen St W, Toronto, ON M5V 1Z4

        Soft White Compressed Mask Sheet Hydration (20 pcs)

        Salmon Sushi Cat Plush Toy 13.7" Cute Stuffed Animal Soft

1:33PM ET—Tim Hortons
  148 Simcoe St • Delivery • 800 points redeemed
    Vanilla Cream Cold Brew (M)
    Blackberry Yuzu Sparkling Quencher (M)
    Smoky Honey Bacon Breakfast Sandwich

1:36PM ET—Google
  "psychiatrist toronto"
  "filipino psychiatrist toronto"
  "disabled psychiatrist toronto"
  "does ohip cover psychiatry"
  "out of pocket cost psychiatry toronto"
  "how to sell kidney"

Anetra Aubade

It's A-N-E-T-R-A, six letters and three vowels.
. . . We don't really have a ballroom culture here in Las Vegas.
A lot of my love for the ballroom scene is just from watching videos on YouTube.
—Anetra, *RuPaul's Drag Race*, season 15

Four AM. Minute studio, a duvet.
Device azures, cornea pierce. Google:
Who am I? Social animal? Exotic facade?

Mature novice. Desire nearby simile people.
Desire houses, mutual belief. Desire reason, please.
But our region remote. Option famine. Meager refuge.

Always inside. Always sedate, behave, career.
Origin enigma. Source myriad degree abroad.
Unable become. Racial errata. Home as isofac.

Forage escape. Forage clique, allies, domain.
Videos Manila. Videos vogues, native tongue.
Pinoys so homosexual. Weirdo libido viable.

O these bodies, feeble, ailing, uneven, impair—and joy,
so also. Purely. Anetra so diva, entire iconic. See her:
see Rob. Steady figure him out: I, bakla, insane, and joy.

Sun. Day awakes. Enough awaits. Choose family online,
dilate trauma radius. Pursue joyous. Pursue values.
Pursue gay and masaya, attain the due ligaya.

Fashion!

Dystopia

We dress to survive deviance.   Weak black organza fabric that is not very
rugged   that refrains from choking you   that will not rough up skin that
cannot handle it.   Acid-wash jeans that are missing part
of the knee   the gap silently filled with scrap metal.   Large pockets for when
you cannot use your hands   but you cannot leave behind anything.
          A blazer with shredded sleeves   garish zippers unable to
be concealed   stuck modulating how much limb absence slips
through   prostheses that never quite look skin-colored.
Gaudy colors of fabric we hack apart   to manage and
distract from our fragile irregularity.   Limping (shameful)   because
you cannot walk steadily   because you have forgotten stability.   Clothes
we swap with one another   because we do not have to the right bodies to swap
with anyone else because our backs could not support those threads.
The garments more graceful than our movement.   Access
as an admission: this is what we must live without.

Utopia

We dress to serve life, diva.   Soft black eleganza fabric that is gentle
that allows you to breathe   that respects the demands of delicate skin.
Acid-wash jeans that have turned the knee   into a percussion instrument
jeans that now sing.   Large pockets for when your hands are
busy enjoying   a cane, a cell phone, a lover.   A blazer with ribboned
sleeves   bold zippers on display   eager to show as
much limb difference as there is   prostheses that no longer worry
about trying to pass as flesh.   Brilliant colors of fabric that we
hack   to mirror and delight in our fabulous intensity.
        Limping (sashaying)   because your body naturally knows
how to   while walking must be learned.   Clothes we swap with one another
because we have the right bodies for each other   because we already carry
each other on our backs.   The garments only graceful because we
move in them.   Access as an aesthetic: this is what we could not
live without.

I Love My Friends

Arin and Rachel take shrooms on the same day
I skip my meds so we can all trip together.

Every time I am sitting with friends on a blanket
at Grange Park at 6PM drinking carton rosé I'm like,

This is what I was born to do.

Every time I am fetal on the plastic disk swing
at 2AM, Gabbie watching from the slide, mumbling
to myself *illegal illegal illegal illegal*, I'm like,

I guess this is also what I was born to do.

I have no photos from these picnics
though I can picture them more clearly than any other part of my life.

These tiny, sacred moments.

I pick Colwill up from the airport, take side streets home so we can keep
the windows down without having to shout our gossip

over the wind. Jody and I giggle non sequiturs in the chat
while the Zoom presenter tries to turn on captions and share

their screen. I apologize to Peter for sleeping until noon during our visit
and he laughs, says my grogginess is the most beautiful thing about me.

This is just what I can remember.

Like Candy

for Tim Dlugos / after "G-9"

I jog calmly, rhythmically, my small legs
extending from the tiny shorts
that I got to draw boys' attention
at the gym. Upon learning that your former
home in New Haven is still standing,
I've decided to run there
on my day off. Eli had left early
that morning, gathering his things
as I brushed my teeth and laid out clothes
for my shift later at the lab. *Have fun
looking at brains all day* and a kiss
before leaving. Last week he had asked me
if I would get on PrEP. *Just to be sure,*
he murmured into my neck as we fell
asleep. I told him I was worried it would
interfere with my other meds but
would check with my doctor. *Would it be
the worst thing if you went a little crazy again
just to fuck me good?* He smiled, a joke only he
could pull off, the eyes-closed grin, his groggy
fingers tapping out bassoon melodies
on my bare hip. The doctor told me
there were no serious interactions between
Descovy and Seroquel, so I went
to the Walgreens on York to pick it up:
pre-exposure prophylaxis. Tim, they are handing out
these pills like candy. Here, look,
see the blue ridges, the smooth
rectangles, how they dissolve like stigmata

and your hands are finally clean. But
they were never dirty, just eager, and joyful,
and young. A clean light flushes across
the side of East Rock in the distance
as I run by the Divinity School. I took
a seminar there with Christian on poetry
and faith. I wish I could say
I felt your spirit moving through
the old hallways, but I am still looking
for you. I am running up Prospect Street
until I find you. I still have the course packet
from the class, and there is an entire section
of poems about joy. Can I read it to you?
I promise I will when I get to you. For now
I keep running, finding my way
through your old neighborhood. When I can
no longer respond with words, I run.
Eli always tells the story of just before
we met when we had been chatting
over Facebook. The afternoon before
our first date (a walk up Science Hill
to sit on the swing outside the observatory)
I was jogging through Cross Campus
and almost crashed into him. *You were going*
too fast for me to move out of the way
or recognize you, but I was just happy
to have a cute boy knock me over, he laughs.
It is stories like this, nostalgia
for a time when love and anxiety didn't weave
so tightly together. And then I remember
that last year's Rob is inside me somewhere.
With every house I pass, I want to gather
a memory of wonder, a sphere

of glowing light I can place
on your doorstep when I get there.
This house is for when Jeff and I
lost our jackets at Industry and walked
twenty blocks in tank tops, hugging
each other, rubbing our arms up
and down and laughing
at the slush in our sneakers.
This house is for last summer's Klonopin
incident, Clay picking up my unconscious
body in the alley outside Roscoe's
and drunkenly trying to wake me up
by holding poppers under my nose
like smelling salts. And this house is for you,
Tim, when Colin introduced us before
we all got on that flight to Minneapolis,
and you had to watch me sob across the aisle
the whole time because I could not believe
Danny would just leave me like that. Or at least
that is how it felt to me, as if you were
really there. You died in 1990, 22 years before
PrEP. I want to tilt your head back
as you lie in G-9 and help you swallow
one down, even if you are too sick already,
if I know it won't help, if my aid
means nothing. You can get a coupon online
for a zero-dollar copay. You don't even need
insurance. We are all on it. Graham makes
a show of taking his with a tequila soda
at Woads, *This is gay culture!* shouted
over a tangle of limbs and Madonna.
Gay people will always love each other
like Death is dancing with us. We will

get him kicked out of the bar then go
eat bodega sandwiches in the park.
Every light-up floor flashes
with the special kind of cherishing
that comes with the end of a plague.
And yes, the plague is not really
over. But we have another
medicine now for those already
positive. It makes the viral load
undetectable, and therefore
untransmittable, the ways we love
each other uncompromising,
the stigma unraveling, our bodies
undulating in the crowd until our love
is understood as a river that glows
every morning, that still flows
with the same strength as before.
Michael and Alan have been together
for eleven years now. I saw them dancing
in Boston with my aunt. Me and Matty
go to Partners on a weeknight, our bodies
warm with whiskey, never weak with thin
blood. On some weekends they even bring in
New York City drag queens for cabaret numbers
at 168 York Street. I'll save a seat for you.
I still call Sachin faking a breakdown every time
he has a bad date. Kevin still finds
a reason to take his shirt off at every
formal party. In the mornings, Eli still
slips pennies into my shoes, *so you have
a lucky run*. And the still light still enters my room
at dawn. It is strange how quickly my legs
wake up, how normal the heat in my muscles

feels. I am making a list of all the boys
I have ever loved and all the boys I know
who have died from the virus. Both lists
are for you. There is no second list.
The list of boys on PrEP is growing
every day. Outside my apartment in Boystown
last summer, the crosswalk was painted
with rainbow stripes that I could almost feel
staying with my body as I passed over them
on my morning run, ribbons of color
wrapping around my legs like bands
of light. That was the summer Eli
and I tried going open, *to manage
the long distance.* That ended quickly, with me
sobbing over the phone after I had
drunkenly invited a neighbor over
and had to kick him out as soon as his hand
grazed my collarbone. Today, Eli and I
worry less about missing out
on debauchery. We stopped wanting to go
to sex parties together once the two
of us spent three days together
in the hospital after some laced coke induced
a more-intense-than-usual psychotic episode.
*Eli, don't just sit here with me, go to class, hurry,
leave me, I'm gonna be crazy forever then die.*
He ate cafeteria mac and cheese and vending-
machine duplex cookies for every
meal so he didn't have to leave
the hospital between visiting hours.
The quiet devastation of realizing
that to your lover, you were never
a monster, never a burden for being

sick. Every day we further loosen the leather
harness that squeezes gay love and death
together. There are no monsters chasing me
on this run, just square after square
of sidewalk, elm after elm, and look—
here I am, outside your old house, and suddenly
I want Eli to be here too, to hold on to,
to take his hand and run it up the banister.
The house is beautiful. The blue paint is worn,
chipping, the same sky blue as the free
pills, as the sunny reality that I ran here
to tell you about. The sides of the house
are streaked with thin vertical stripes
of rain rot, just like the pinstripe curtains
in your hospital room, the drapes
and sheets at your P-town guesthouse.
I have never been there, but I will get
to go—maybe next summer, with Eli,
I hope, if we are still together,
not just if he is still alive, because
he will be, Tim—we both will be.
And I will keep running for you.
I will stay by the side of my gay
friends and lovers to anthologize
each colored light, toothy grin,
messy desire. I will put it all in a book
for you, and on the sky-blue cover
I will cross out *G-9* and etch in
GSI 225, shape it like a small
oblong capsule so that it is like
you are holding the cure itself in your hands
when you are reading this poem,

this poem about joy.
And here is our graceful
exposure, and here is the love persistent,
as I kneel, sobbing, like I always do,
outside your house, where we are
supposed to be, the morning light
wild on my skin as it breaks, over
and over again, each mote of glow
lifting me, cell by cell—
I am glowing. Your whole house
is glowing. It is 6AM, Tim.
I am running to you.

Exit: Gift Shop and Vestibule

Checkout

Where Does Joy Live in the Body

Original artwork: Feel free to look.

1. At the department dinner, I drink too much and spill
   to Heather about my body dysmorphia. She nods, then
   shrugs and laughs, carefree: *It's great to be blind.*

2. I get indecisive trying to choose the most perfect avocado
   while making lunch with Lorraine. When I ask for her help
   she stares, gives me a wry smile. *They all feel the same to my hands.*

3. Alex witnesses my descent into psychobabble as we walk
   each other home from Lee's Palace after the Joy Division tribute concert.
   The next day, they text: *Lol, you made me doubt that I could read lips.*

4. When I offer Leah one of my Oreos, she perks up, holds
   the cookie to her nose, closes her eyes as she inhales. *I can't handle
   the taste, but eventually I fell in love with the smell. Small wins, you know?*

Multisensory replica: Feel free to touch, listen, taste, smell.

1.   the   art   and

      the   body

        are

              perfect

    witnesses   to

each other   's   Joy

         yes

    even   *you*

Souvenir replica: Feel free to take home with you.

artbody perfect
witness each other
joy yes you

How To Survive

after Kate Baer

1. Stop doing it just because it is all there is to do,
   though this does not mean there will be other

2. Things to do: Choose a part of yourself to let rot
   so you may lovingly call it rotten. Try not to

3. Panic. That's part of this. Come have a soda with me
   and panic. Let's talk sleep hygiene, why you tend to

4. Romanticize your survival—it's okay. That's actually also
   part of the process, except for when it can completely

5. Work against the cause. You can microdose depression
   to activate care, which sounds insane, and it is; still, try it,

6. Be just sad enough to recognize that if you are going to love
   being alive, then those knots inextricably tied to your life

7. You must love: illness, devastation, malaise. Think of this
   less as living a life and more as a silly challenge to

8. Outlast yourself with yourself. Decide to not always be okay—
   you are a creature. You need rhythms. You need to

9. Dance. Dance anywhere that forces you toward
   company, or dance alone, dance even when you can't

10. Leave the house. As you walk to the mini-mart, allow that small tickle of mundane detachment so you might

11. Cling to life more tightly. Remember that every *Doesn't feel good* exists in the same world as every

12. *Feels good*—let it. The wrongness never leaves your side, it loves you, it stays, how could you not do the same?

Bench

Eli Tidies Up

And when you have rinsed my spoon for the last time
I hope you feel you have earned your rest
though you always say rest is not something that must be earned
for me I hope you make one more exception

Notes

The French artist mentioned in "We Do Not Enter the Gallery" is Aristide Maillol.

"Access Cues" is modeled after social cues used by artist Salima Punjani.

The ending of "Commute" is after Leila Chatti's "Angel."

"Maid" is written in reference to Canada's MAiD (Medical Assistance in Dying) policy, which has recently been expanded to include individuals managing mental illness/disability. The poem also references "Musée des Beaux Arts" by W. H. Auden.

"Nature Poem" is for Gabrielle Grace Hogan and Kurt David.

"History of Display" and "Access Rider" are after Chessy Normile.

"At Tangled" is written about Tangled Art + Disability, a disability arts gallery in Toronto, Ontario.

"Hopescrolling" includes many real tweets and TikToks as well as many fictional posts: @jimmyjan @CalltoActivism @scarlet_may.1 @ft.jessika.main @annaboebana @ouchnorin @jennaxhealth @theleighton @nauseatedsarah

@tonimorganxx @elliebleach @matthewandpaul @alex1leg @malnurishedrat @nyceeclipz @McDonalds @ang22la.

In "Access Rider," an access rider refers to a list of access needs one provides to a work partner prior to beginning work together, similar to riders that many celebrities use.

"God Is in the Gallery" draws inspiration from Acts 9:16–18 and from the performance artist Marina Abramović.

"Empty Frame for the Artist Who Was Too Sick to Ever Finish the Work or Make It to the Gallery" draws inspiration from Tangled's exhibition *Undeliverable*, which opened without artist statements as an unplanned gesture toward crip time.

The interpreter referred to in "Eli Interprets" is Marc Ethan, who interprets Auslan. The poem also modifies a line from Sylvia Plath.

The title of "The Body Is Not an Apology Except for Mine Sometimes" refers to *The Body Is Not an Apology* by Sonya Renee Taylor.

The art show mentioned in "Self-Portrait Without Sense of Self" combines features from the shows *avere cura* at Tangled and *Paleta 35* by the Philippine Artists Group of Canada.

The eponym of "Seafood City" is a Filipino grocery store chain.

"Anetra Aubade" is an anetra, an invented form consisting of six tercets composed entirely of units of six letters, three of which are vowels.

"Fashion!" describes the disabled fashion show *Cripping Masculinity* held at 401 Richmond in Toronto and draws from the event script, read aloud in person by Ben Barry and Kristina McMullin. The title is drawn from Lady Gaga's track of the same name on her 2013 album *ARTPOP*.

"Like Candy" was written for the poet Tim Dlugos in response to his poem "G-9." As mentioned in the poem, Tim died of AIDS in 1990, twenty-two years before the approval of the HIV-prevention drug PrEP.

"Eli Tidies Up" is after Jackson Holbert.

Acknowledgments

So many hands have been all over this book, whether or not they could feel it. Utter and abundant thanks to the following.

To the journals below in which a number of these poems first appeared, often in earlier versions.

The American Poetry Review: "Abecedarian for the Care Shift I Failed to Show Up For" and "Commute"

Booth: "Maid"

The Capilano Review: "The Softness of Language"

Diode: "History of Display" and "Hopescrolling"

The Ex-Puritan: "The Friending of Burden" and "omfg"

Four Way Review: "A Case for Self-Harm"

Gulf Coast: "Nature Poem" (as "Virtue")

Hayden's Ferry Review: "Eli Interprets"

The Journal: "Self-Portrait and Tactile Replica as Living Ghost"

Journal of Arts and Communities: "Access Legend," "Access Guide," "Information," "Access Cues," "Sensory Room," "Fine Art," "Artist Talk," "Three Translations of an Email to My Boss," "Empty Frame for the Artist Who Was Too Sick to Ever Finish the Work or Make It to the Gallery," "I Need a Minute," "God Is in the Gallery," and "Where Does Joy Live in the Body"

Los Angeles Review: "I Love My Friends"

Malahat Review: "On Sex"

The Margins (Asian American Writers' Workshop): "Anetra Aubade" and "Hardly Creatures"

The Missouri Review: "We Do Not Enter The Gallery"

MQR Mixtape: Place: "Seafood City"

New England Review: "Ode to Pissing" and "Therapist"

North American Review: "Abecedarian After Forgetting Yesterday's Medication"

Pleiades: "Hôpital des Beaux Arts"

Poet Lore: "Fashion!"

Salamander: "How to Survive"

The Sewanee Review: "At Tangled"

Shenandoah: "The Body Is Not an Apology Except for Mine Sometimes"

Sixth Finch: "Eli Eats Dirt" and "Eli Invents"

Tammy: "Like Candy" (reprinted at Poets.org)

To the entire team at Tin House, especially my editor Alyssa Ogi, for the endless generosity and grace with my work. What joy to be part of this family.

To Gabrielle Grace Hogan: none of these poems would be possible without your unfailing support, your keen eye, and our simpler times.

To my other first readers, Jody Chan and Kurt David, for walking these halls while the paintings were still scattered across the floor. Jody, I am always ready to talk about "it." Kurt, I am always ready to lend you clothes.

To my New Writers Project family—Colwill Brown, Ellaree Yeagley, Juan Fernando Villagómez—who knew this book would exist long before I did.

And to the rest of my peers in Austin whose words laid the groundwork for this book years before it materialized, especially ChiChi Abii, Amanda Bestor-Siegal, Maryan Nagy Captan, Laurel Faye, Shaina Frazier, Sanjana Thakur, and Molly Williams.

To Tangled and everyone there, Jet Coghlan, Nicole Crawford, Max Ferguson, Jack Hawk, Sean Lee, Madi Lekei, Heidi Persaud, and Cyn Rozeboom, for being the physical and emotional inspiration behind this entire project. And to the larger disability arts community in Canada, especially Workman Arts and the Dreaming Otherwise workshop.

To my professors at UT Austin who encouraged me even when I had no idea what I was writing about and no urgency to figure it out: Chad Bennett, Jennifer Chang, Carrie Fountain, Alison Kafer, Joanna Klink, Elizabeth McCracken, Lisa Olstein, Roger Reeves, Natasha Trethewey, and Nick Winges-Yanez. To my earlier professors, especially Claudia Rankine, Emily Skillings, and Amanda Nadelberg, who convinced me to do the poetry thing in the first place. And to Elizabeth Wagenschutz, for everything.

To everyone at the Toronto Metropolitan University School of Disability Studies, who generously hosted me while on Fulbright. Special thanks to my adviser Eliza Chandler, who took on my project when it was nothing other than desperation to find crip community.

To MacDowell, for the freedom to create. Special love to Amara Janae Brady and Cesario Lavery for completing our queer trinity.

To the Kenyon Review Writers Workshop, Leila Chatti, and all the inimitable squonks, for letting me know that these were poems. Special love to my sibling Pınar Banu Yaşar: may we always be loud.

To the editorial team at *Foglifter*, especially my poetry coconspirators Luiza Flynn-Goodlet, MJ Jones, Charlie Neer, and Dior Stephens, for keeping things so very gay. To the reader and editorial team at *Poetry*, for every conversation that helped me to keep the faith in poems and poets even as larger institutions failed us.

To Jane Wong and my peers in her winter workshop at Tin House, who caught this book at the tail end of its search for a home yet supported it as if they had known it its whole life.

To Chris Martin, who believed in my work before any of these poems were even seeds.

To my entire family, especially my mom, dad, and kuya, for believing in poetry simply because they believed in me.

To everyone else: Arin Bennett, Allison Bradshaw, Elaine Cagulada, Chen Chen, Adrienne Chung, Peter Chung, Katie Condon, Ryan Craver, Carolina Đỗ, Colin Drohan, Loree Erickson, Miggy Esteban, Róisín Goebelbecker, Sam Grabiner, Zainab Hussein, Jennie Livingston, Rachel Lucas, Bebe Miller, Diana Khoi Nguyen, Jeff Nytch, Sachin Peddada, Kevin Renn, Audrey San Diego, Catherine St. Hilaire, Juliana Upchurch, and Tree Williams. And to everyone whose name I couldn't squeeze here—know that I squeezed it into my heart.

To my crip kin whom I have known and whom I will know and whom I will never know again, this book is for you.

To Levi: I love you. I promise this is the last page and now I will rest.

Rob Macaisa Colgate is a disabled, bakla, Filipino American poet from Evanston, Illinois. A 2025 National Endowment for the Arts Fellow, he received an MFA in poetry and critical disability studies from UT Austin. Poems from this collection appear or are forthcoming in *American Poetry Review, Sewanee Review, Best New Poets, New England Review, The Margins*, and elsewhere. A former Fulbright scholar, Rob currently serves as the managing poetry editor at *Foglifter*.